a destination
is only as good
as those who are
traveling to find it.

here's to the lost
ones who make
the most out of
the unknown.

my muse, you are all
things beautiful and
without you, i still
wouldn't know
myself.

-z.k.d

Where We Go From Here

By Zachry K. Douglas

i know how much you love your life and how hard it
has been trying to go to sleep and wake up with a smile.
it tells me a story about a woman who had been lost for
a little while and then finally found a glimpse of herself
that she loved. it tells me how much she loves to travel
and isn't satisfied with what life has given her yet.

she isn't lost, because she's a born wanderer who enjoys
being alone at times to hear the things others cannot.
it also tells me how big her heart is and how lovely a
soul she has. it tells me she is nervous about talking
about a future with someone when she is happy with
what she has now. she questions life, not on everything,
but the issues that truly matter. she loves colorful
objects and obviously loves to read to gain the
knowledge countless others say they don't have
time for.

she loves finding the hidden gems in a world which has
killed many by trying to be their best self. there is nothing
more beautiful than someone who opens their heart to
somebody they feel worthy of loving. it is a tragic play,
set in an era of hate and repressed feelings, but she has a
way of bringing out the best in people and they feel
comfortable taking off their masks to feel the sun
for the first time. wherever you find yourself,
i hope it is next to someone like her.

if only these words

could've found you

sooner, then maybe

your presence

wouldn't feel so

empty.

i

find

myself

in

every

word

you

never

said.

we laugh and love like

    the seas of yesterday,

        but we forget how to

            get back there like

                sailors without a

                    lighthouse to

                        show them

                            where to

                                  go.

we toss and turn
between the
innocence
of what we
have lost
and what
we have
found.

crumbs of the
light before
us, we go
in search
of
wholeness.

we all come and go in this life. some leave us with memories and others take anything they can get their dirty hands on. there are times i cannot even remember my name or what i actually look like, but i act like i know what i'm doing. reluctantly, we scour for truth amongst the barren fields of love, thinking we can find all of the answers. there's hesitation laced with fear, and yet we continue on because deep down we feel that there has to be a reason for this pain wrapped around our bodies like clothes that don't fit. it can bring us down to the bottom of the earth's feet. the ones that trample over us without worrying about the consequences.

sometimes we are not crushed by the force itself, but the words of which are never said. we all come and go in this life, but what we choose to leave behind for others to learn from will be our legacy.

be a smile for someone who has never known of one before. be a laugh for someone who has always been laughed at because they were different.

at the end of the day, just be kind and gentle to the wild around you. all of the life you see is precious and it deserves your very best.

though she may get on
my nerves more than i
would like to admit,

she loves me
unconditionally.

even when she knows
nothing about this
world, she loves
me.

not because she is
supposed to,
but because
she knows
my heart.

we all hope to find peace within a single breath.

even when it's hard to breathe, the chaos feeds

the wild and beauty feeds the soul.

find yours and grow freely in all of the places

that make you insanely happy to be yourself.

to those who

have seen the

sun and tasted

its warmth,

we are from the

same breath.

we are called upon
to find what makes
our hearts crazy

and

what brings passion
to our front door.
when it knocks,
open and welcome
the madness you've
always needed.

when the sky falls,
look for the stars
still holding on by
the threads of the
universe.

those are the ones
who are brave
enough to
call
chaos
home.

friends are people who
know your soul and fight
to keep it safe, no matter
how far away they are.

they are the relentless
peace keepers for
those who call on
them.

there's a story about
how the moon got its
glow.

they say when the sun
kissed the universe,
the stars gave a
piece of themselves
away so he could
find her again.

we love like fighters
struggling to stay on
our feet. we live as if
our fingertips have
fire on the ends of
them. we laugh like
there is a kind of
happiness we used to
know living down there.
we hardly ever make sense,
but the universe never makes
mistakes.

> <u>you matter and everything you
> do from this point forward is
> a light for others.</u>

we walk though life
unaware of the beauty
we see and oftentimes
when we go back to
try and visualize it,
it's gone.

take time to see the roses
growing out of your soul,
so you can learn to
appreciate the
times when blooming is
the only thing we know
how to do when
winter takes away
from our growth.

wandering on this world,
we shall continue to travel
until our bones know where
home is.

somewhere underneath the
sky, blankets of stars shall
unfold and light will warm
the parts of your soul
that had once been
lost.

we grow by the sun and love by the sea,

but where we are destined for is between

the breath of a falling leaf.

a journey is where we lead

ourselves when the path in

front of our hearts is

blocked.

the mood changes, but the

scenery is medicine for the

soul.

they say it's about the
people in our lives when
we think all else is gone.

never forget the ones who
stayed when you thought
you yourself would leave
who you are.

there is a light inside
of you the moon is
jealous of and the
stars smile at,
even during
the day.

never dim it for anyone.

lucky for us all,

nature gives us

the best poetry

there is.

no need to write.

just listen.

we fall for stars.
we rise for ourselves.
we live for laughter.
we hope for miracles.
we breathe in dreams.
we breathe out memories.
we love who we love.
no matter how far away we
are, light will always hit us
in the wild no one else can
see.

a single breath can
change the way we
create the magic
around us.

breathe in your destiny
and build endlessly,
together, forever.

we learn at an early age
that we have the power
to be whoever we want.
whether it is a superhero,
ballerina, fireman, doctor,
lawyer, or just someone
who isn't afraid of loving.
be brave with it and give it
all you have. we only get
one chance at living.

be meaningful and fight to own it.

there is a reason why we
fall and rise with the sun.
there's a reason why we
sway and swim with the
oceans.

       we hope that it will carry
       us to where we need to
       be loved.

my face is melting from the sun. there's no shelter from
the heat. no place i can run. i am angry and left wondering
if i am the reason for my own demise. pieces of tears have
followed me into this world i am living now.

       maybe the rain will fall and cleanse me of
       these memories peppered to my bones.

she's a

fallen

angel

wrapped

in sin,

with a

power

to love,

and begin

again.

break open and love yourself.

the beginning only asks that

from you.

let it out.

as bad as

it hurts,

let it out.

the moon does it every night.

when you feel it,
become it.

someday, it might
make you brave
enough to
believe
it.

the ocean carries more
than the waves of those
making dreams come
true.

it carries the hearts of
lovers hoping to reach
the shore before it's
too late.

up, up and away,
rising to meet the
moon to tell her
about the day.

love has a way of
letting go right
before you
want it to.

our lives were meant to taste
the freedom and hear and
see the love around us.

don't hold back when it comes
to living.

find that next adventure and go
with your entire soul.

life does not give out second chances.
it only tells you the truth behind the
lies so many never want to hear.

wander amongst the stars
and find a place you feel
understands the wild
inside of your bones.

once you do, thank them
and tell them your story.

don't worry, they will listen.
wanderers understand each
other better than those who
think they know themselves.

do not settle for anything
or anyone. that's for the
dust and fog around us.
be patient, but bold in
everything that sets
your soul free.

    find that, and you will see
    what you have been
    missing out on this
    whole time you
    thought it
    couldn't
    get any
    better.

there's a place we
all must go before
it's too late.

be love and hold steady.

there's great work to be
done outside of our skin
and it all starts from
within.

everything around
you is what we need,
even when there's no
hope.

the music, oceans, songs, friends,
adventures, and the moon are the
priceless pieces of art that moves
the soul inside of you.

keep flying, and just be.

the best kind of humans
are the one who get to
know you and want to
stay even after you've
left yourself more
times than you
can remember.

just breathe

in a little

more life

   and

write down

your dreams,

not in ink,

but in stars.

we go where we
are needed and
the universe calls
out to everyone.

press your soul
against the sky
and react.

wherever you go,
go with all of your
soul, heart, mind,
and being.

when you arrive,
plant yourself
there and water
daily.

don't wait for others
when we are destined
to bloom by loving
ourselves.

may we all get to the point
in our lives where we care
enough for ourselves and
find happiness in the
laughter around us and
inside of us.

call me crazy if you'd like,
but there's more i want
from this place and i don't
feel like it will ever satisfy
my sickness.

there are no mistakes
when it comes to life.
the best way to get out
of a situation is to break
through whatever is holding
you back.

>full heart.
>all soul.
>all the time.

there's a place where

all the lost go. a place

in the wild of your soul.

follow the signs and be

free upon reaching your

full potential.

there's no sense in rushing
the moon to rise or the stars
to shine brighter;

we all find our way in the end.
some just enjoy the moments
longer.

continue down the road
until you are seeing the
mountains ahead,
the ocean beside you,
and the sun raining down
on you.

always keep to the wild side.

i would be honored
if you wore the flowers
i picked for you in your
hair.

nothing is as beautiful
as a bouquet of happiness
when it is on display by love
itself.

however the stars fall
and rise again in the
sky above you, may they
always find their way home.

may we all become lost and
find ourselves where we need
to be.

stay as long as you can and never
overthink the possibility of becoming
mad. we all are anyways.

some just choose to believe it rather
than pretending to be normal.

we are the restlessness

settling down by the sunset,

waiting for the universe to

bring us to the dreams we

desperately are in search of.

time allows us
the gift to visit
memories and
gives our hearts
the chance to
settle when the
moment calls
upon us to
remember who
we are when it
matters the
most.

life is about the unknown,

but still, we try our best to

act as if we understand the

parallels between the love

we want and the love we

need.

i woke up with a beast inside
of me, a wolf beside me, and
a mad world around me.

all of which are fighting to be
free before time becomes
deceased.

above all things,
seek love in the
sincerest of forms

and

learn what you want
on the other-side
of your heart.

for those who are fortunate
enough to know you and to
the ones who have yet to see
the moon and sun dance
around you, keep shining.

unique souls are a treasure without a map.

this road you're on,
be sure to appreciate
the sounds around you
and breathe in as much
as sun as you can.

fill yourself with hope before
letting go of those who try
to keep you in the sky.

the things we see are only
there long enough for you
to understand what they
mean to you.

if you're lucky, some will stay
with you forever and teach
you that it's okay to be
strange.

may you close your eyes and see
the magic you are capable of
making, only to open your
eyes and witness tiny
miracles throughout
your day.

    we are what we love.
    we are where our
    heart is.

        hold them both
        gently as you
        go.

though we all will stumble,

we will always have the ability

to stand again, because the

soul inside of our bodies was

not made to rest in one place

for too long.

we look to others
for safety when
we have been
protecting what
everyone wants.

we are the guards.

she gave me all i would

need when she smiled

back at me;

making the sun rise

again.

what's meant to
be won't always
be there.

you will have to
move eventually.

we look up to see how small we really are in
this life, but there are some things that no
matter the time or location always appear
bigger than the world we are living in.

        sometimes, it's all heart
        and other times it's all
        soul, but always trust
        in both.

the story doesn't have

to make sense. just be

who you want and let

the rest write itself.

through the fire, my soul was made
and through the oceans surrounding
yours, i will brave the depths to breathe
the universe again.

may we welcome in the new you
as you go on the adventure of
finding who you are.

no matter what's in
front of you or how
far you have left to
travel,

a deep breath can make
you do incredible things.
sometimes, it may be the
only thing that separates
you from being your
own worst enemy.

across the oceans you
will find every star that
had once fallen for a
dream to kiss the
waves.

it's not a burial.
it's called sacrifice.

follow

    your

        own

            path

        and

    watch

        the

            flowers

                grow.

i love you, and you are my world.

within it, you have walked with

me without ever letting go.

thank you for making sure i feel

each touch your soul allows me

to have.

we feel so much

because pain

is only meant to

teach us.

not kill us.

there comes a time in
our life when nothing
will make sense or feel
right, but it's okay.

not everything is supposed
to work out the way you
think.

some of us just keep moving
despite never knowing
anything at all.

we go where we are called upon,

and wherever that place is located,

belong to it with all of who you are.

make it a home you will be proud of.

life is too precious to
waste on those who
treat you ordinary
and vanilla.

treat yourself to all of
the universal flowers
in each sunrise and
sunset.

taste the truth in your
heart before moving
forward.

we reached our hands

towards the sky and

pulled down every star

we could see.

now take my hand and bring

to life the constellations we

had heard about and make

them wild once again.

we must first decide what

it is we are after and then

set our sails and open our

hearts to arrive at the soul

of the destination.

we ride high without fear of

slowing down, because we

are the night.

there comes a point in our
lives where closing our eyes
can only get us so far.

see the wonders and become
the adventures you seek.

go now and revel in awe.
it's your right to be
captivated.

do not be afraid of the
darkness many have
tried to put you in.

for you are brilliant
and were made from
all of the things
cosmos and
star-like.

life teaches us many things,

but the most important one

is love for ourselves.

like the trees in the winter,

it may get lonely, but if we

continue to love who

we are, summer will

kiss our souls once

again.

throughout our walks and despite the aches our hearts endure at times, the universe granted the stars to shine regardless of the pain.

sometimes we must appreciate the things we have no control over, in order to love again.

some walk.

some run.

some crawl.

some fly.

some swim.

we all die trying

to get to where

we feel our wild

be free.

whether you realize

    it or not, someone

        right now is looking

            for your smile to save

                their life.

there's a wave out in the
ocean that is on its way
to the shore.

it doesn't ask questions.
it just moves forward
without fear of time
and space.

it goes whether its unsteady
or not. it goes and survives
because believing is half
the battle.

our eyes see things our hearts
have always known. be sure you
feel all there is to embrace before
you decide to let go. once you do,
never look back.

there isn't anything for you.

shadows are supposed to stay
behind to remind us we are the
light coming out of the universe
and we demand to be seen for
who we are now.

when you look at yourself,

i hope you see the

inspiration you've

always been to

others.

dreams fuel our souls for
the destination. they give
our hearts the burning
images inside the cages
they are kept.

      don't be afraid to
      chase your destiny.

it's your right to be there.

we fight for the things
we never want to lose.

make yourself one of
those and you will
never be without.

there's a light inside of you

that if you listen close enough,

you will hear the stars needing

to be released on their journey.

at the end of the day, we are
only responsible for how we
treated ourselves and those
who walked on our path.

some will stay and others
will continue going forward.
aspire to find happiness in
everything that blooms with
fire.

there are days where i feel
the weight of every single
lovely star inside of my chest,
yet i move as if i was flying
next to them. i am filled with
too much love to feel nothing
for the chaos that lives with me
and my demons.

to
those
who
dream,
may
you
never
waste
a
single
star.

we believe there is more
to life than opening our
eyes to see a sun rising
and a moon in every
phase.

and if that it is all some
of us get, it is more than
most.

      be kind.

      be love.

may the sky open so you
can see the path in front
of you.

may the water be
kind to your soul.

we go as far as the lungs
inside of us can expand
to reach.

prepare your breath for
the journey.

you will need each one
where you are going.

there's great release in
the cosmos as you
tear away from
who you used
to be.

    become the universe you
    were meant to thrive in.

the light will always drive out

the darkness, until it realizes

it only exists to become the

stars inside who fear the

open spaces between

hope and pain.

the day will come to where
we lay our weapons down
and pick up where we left
off.

but the war is us, and we
are the fire; forever burning
with pride.

we go where the sun leads us
and where the moon sees us.

go now and rest your heart
on her light.

be like water
for those who
need it;

    surround them completely.

    save them entirely.

    love them with softness.

    heal them from the inside.

there is great joy in the abandonment
of fear despite the chaos surrounding
you.

embrace everything that makes you feel
alive. let go of what does not. we are our
own garden of life.

there is only love in
the space between
the universe and the
stars.

      if you cannot see it, become it.

to be able to breathe
is luxury so many tend
to hold in,

when we must let it go.

thank you for bringing your heart everywhere you go.

it is a sight needed by many to know what exactly we

are living for.

i think about you more than i probably should,
but i have been told in the past that you
should always tell the people who are
in your life how much they are
loved and appreciated.

> i haven't been good at that throughout my life.
> not because i am a bad person, but for the simple
> reason of being shy towards most of them. i am
> getting better, especially with you. i want you to
> know how much i care about you and i want
> nothing but the best for you.

you are everything i
had imagined before

and

everything i need more
of. a taste of you and i
lose myself completely.
and i can only wait
patiently until i have
you again.

you and i have collected

the ashes of who we used

to be, and yet, still light

matches to burn the dark.

there's me, then there's who
i am with you. my heart had
been caged since the day i
kissed the world around me.

you, my dear, you have
allowed me a freedom
only known to the
springs that flow
underneath the
caves of which
house dreams
for the lonely.

she could set me on fire
with the way her hands
danced on my thigh;

inching closer to where
she always wanted to
go and where i would
always tell her,
"don't stop."

we love with hearts of tomorrow
          and
souls of another lifetime.

when you find your voice, don't be
timid with it.

you have traveled an entire cycle of
pain and refuge to be you.

         break the walls down.

search within

the chaos and

you'll discover

your wild.

don't go through life
expecting the clouds
to give way to you.

make your own light,
even if the darkness
is your friend.

your lips tell me so much

in the way they quiver,

as if they know what's

coming,

but are still afraid of how

you will let yourself feel

when you're with me.

go where you
feel the love
in the roots

and

branches of
the universe.

continue growing.

and if i
have
anything,
i want it to
be with you.
i breathe in,
and i feel
you in the
places i
forgot
needed
air.

until you break,

you don't know

how it feels.

be gentle with

your pieces.

you will need

them later.

may

you

always

find

the wild

in

the

places

you love.

there will be people
who think you have
nothing to offer to
this world.

smile back at those
who do and continue
being the universe
you are.

everyone will be able
to see your stars and
the two moons
beaming out
of your
face.

don't fear the waters
around you. they are
only as deep as you
make them out to be.

swim through it and
dive as often as you
can.

down there you will
find life.

sometimes, you will need to
cannonball into adversity.

we are

the stars

no one sees,

but

we are the

bravest

because we

dare to see

ourselves.

what is set out before
you is a wonderful
display of life and
love.

we see what we want
and i hope when you
look out amongst it
all,

you see a place of
opportunity and
hope.

you are very much the
epitome of how
the world
around
you is.

throw your soul into it
and everything you
do, and be like a
proud parent as
you watch it
grow.

don't try so hard that
you lose yourself in
the process.

be the flower that
blooms in a field
of the most
wildest
things
under
the
stars.

where we are going,

hearts need to

breathe and souls

need to sing.

remain your best-self.

the love we all search for in this life,

is hidden behind the very flesh and

bones we are all made of.

                      it's okay to keep digging.

wherever your heart sings,
don't be shy to scream
out the lyrics to your
song.

it was made to fight for
what you love and it's
the strongest star
inside of you.

a handful of your hair
and your eyes looking
back at me.

this is a place of freedom.

a place of sin.

a place where i kneel

and worship the soul

in you.

i see you too, sweet one.

if i could be closer to you, i'd whisper in your ear the ways in which i want you and how i would please you, step by step. standing naked in front of you, i take your hand and place it over my heart, then move it down my body slowly, until you feel what you do to me. moving closer to you, my chest firmly against your breasts, i kiss your lips so deeply i feel every fear you ever had. we would dance to the wall and i'd take your hands and place them above your head and tell you to only let them fall when you cannot hold them up any longer. my hands glide down your body, cupping your magic and feeling all of the things i've craved since you've been away. our minds drift constantly to every fantasy we wished upon and we stimulate our hearts by the pure rush of innocence we feel by being ourselves with one another. you and i are separated by what seems like eternity, but soon we will know the inevitable of what's been awaiting us since the first time we spoke about nothing, but knowing it meant everything.

i have tried to explain this to you before, so let me do better. my heart races as i wait for your breath to release what i am needing. my skin feels your nails before they even touch me, and i ache to be marked by you. my eyes have never been so open before, as i look at you, trying to move from underneath me. my hands move up from your breasts, to your throat to feel your moans grow louder.
i see you in every room of my mind and you have taken over my entire soul. but here's the secret:

i had long surrendered before you even knew who i was and before i knew who you were. you had me all of this time at your fingertips, and all it took was moving your index finger to get my attention.

from the ashes we

will rise like a

thousand fires

catching the

universe's

flame to

forever

burn

with

the

sun.

we often wonder how
the sky can hold all
the stars we wish
on and how big
are hearts
actually
are.

if you ever find yourself
in doubt of anything,
look up, then search
within.

we hold all of the answers
we try and discover by
asking someone who
doesn't even know
how the moon
makes them
feel.

we go through life with
hopes of finding a pair
of hands that know how
to hold a fragile soul,
looking for solace and
comfort from someone
who has seen us before
we knew how badly we
had been in pain.

thank you for being that
someone, sweet woman.

there's a sound the heart

makes when it is embraced

by love. may you hear this

sound for the rest of your

life.

my goal is to be the best
version of myself and if i
cannot be that,

then i will help someone
else become that for
themselves.

we are better than what
tries to divide us.

walk without fear.

fly without limits.

hope without worry.

live without hating.

love without boundaries.

see everything as you

want it to be and you

will have all you'll need.

we fight to survive
and the only time
that isn't the case
is when you are
dust and free to
live and love as
you please.

never take anything
for granted. even the
sun knows how to
make you miss
the moon.

all life is made up of magic.
believe in yourself and you
will have every ounce of
power it takes to create
something uniquely
your own.

don't get caught up paying
attention to the wrong pair
of hands and miss what you
deserve.

what lies behind the curtain,
is oftentimes your own
insecurities.

a heartbeat shows us how
strong we really are.

regardless of what you face in
life, hold your hand over
your chest and feel it
fighting for you.

now, go out with purpose.

    <u>hold your victory.</u>

we all are from a
time and place
where the heart
sings and the
soul dances.

sometimes, we get
lost and find how
difficult a smile can
be when all we want
to do is lay with our
tears and comfort
them.

somewhere,

    she's still searching
    for the girl she used
    to be.

i was one of the lucky ones.
if it were not for you and my
family, i would either be
dead, or on the streets.

<u>we never know how we are
to be used, until we think
we are all used up.</u>

oftentimes, we forget the true meaning
of self-worth, and end up settling for the
discount others try and give us.

we deserve their best and our best.

we owe ourselves that much, because at
the end of the day, we only get this feeling
of being alive once.

don't waste it on being or feeling ordinary.

in life, learn how to occupy
each day by filling your heart
with treasures you find along
the way.

one can never pick enough stars
or sunsets.

no matter what they try
and tell us, some were
meant to fall in love
with everything,
all at once.

while others were meant
to seek out the shelter
along the way.

perception is more than
just reality, it is love
slapping you in the
face to tell you it
has arrived and
it is up to you
whether or
not you
acknowledge
it.

live the moments that
forever take your breath
away and you will become
a legend to the stars above
you who have yet to find
themselves lost for
something they
love.

go where the animal
in you calls.

fight with the monsters
holding you back from
your destiny.

break free and relish in
greatness.

it is a place for both
sinners and saints.

stay

forever

in the

heart

of

everything

wild and brave.

chapters of our lives
have yet to be written.

don't allow someone
the power to create
and destroy as they
go.

take your life and make
art so you can see true
beauty come to light.

never misplace your truth
and always hold your
ground.

go to your roots as often as you
can without anyone taking you
down.

we look up to see
everything that
allows us the gift
of dreaming.

most of the time
we forget where
home is and
become
wanderers for
something more.

never neglect your star.

there's great reward in doing
something for yourself without
asking anyone to do it.

break open your mind and allow
your dreams to manifest and grow
wildly in the gardens in the sky.

respect your choice and your love.

it is vital to your longevity.

venture out of your comfort
zone from time to time.

nothing spontaneous and
eventful will ever be found
if you don't.

you might end up never coming
back and that will be the day you
find yourself becoming the human
who has longed for the chance to
breathe freely without the support
of someone else's lungs.

she's the rain on the roof that
puts me to sleep and brings
peace into my heart.

the slow sensation of morning
dew on my soul, and i am alive
again to see her sun fall softly
on my chest.

i am at an utter loss for words,
so i will let the blood drip onto
the paper and see what kind
of miracle can come from
sacrificing the soul for the
betterment of my art.

i've never been that successful. i've had success,
but not as much as i expected from myself.
there are better people than me in that area and
i am okay with that. i won't ever own a company.
i'll never run a business of marching suits.
i'll never kiss ass to get to where i need to be,
and i am okay with that.

i am a part of something greater though; my own future.
i am in control and i will not fail. the captain always goes
down with his vessel and this soul wasn't made to sink.
whatever the ocean whispers to me, we speak the same
language. i come from the sea and i am the unrelenting
waves harboring in the darkness.

                    and i am okay with that.

within that moment,
a thousand lifetimes
were changed because
of a single goodbye.

at times, it's hard to
hear a heart break,
when your own soul
is shattering.

i wanted to write something poetic. something that could explode the universe and create a new dimension of reality. "i love you" is what i will type, because i do. even when my ashes are spread into the drifting waters of tomorrow, those who come across the life in the sea, will always see the love i have for you. it is in the way they continue to swim no matter how strong the current they are fighting gets.

it took being a boy to understand the vast realms of life.
it took being a man to see everything in life is that from
a pair of child's eyes. i have seen things. i have lived
through and prevailed from the depths of the deepest
craters that one can create for himself. all it takes is an
understanding that through the constant madness circling
us, we may grow older and our eyes my deceive us, but it's
what we find within us while digging that keeps hope alive.

if i get to hold you
in this life or the
next,

my soul felt your
shine and my
blood is finally
warm again.

after everything i have been through,
i hope this time the universe gave
me the right signs.

love and mirrors
have a lot in
common.

not everything
appears to be
what you
actually
see.

humans and souls are such contradicting animals. one does something for the greater good, while the other does everything based off of feeling greater for themselves. one has a heart and the other has empty bones comprised of broken promises. until you align yourself, with yourself, it will always be a constant battle.

don't get it twisted,
i am a romantic.

one that loves the
very intricate ways
intimacy laces
souls together,

but i also enjoy gently
grabbing your throat
as i take my teeth
and bite the spots
in need of loving.

and if forever should find us, i hope it understands
how long i have been walking this maddening trail
of heartache and loss to find you. i hope it will
allow me to be greedy with you and spoil you every
chance i get. i need forever to know that you and i
are lovers of each other that never gave up their
beliefs to find the peace of knowing what real love
actually feels like.

                    so please, sweet one, let me love you.

she is a dangerous creature.
one that was made from the
ocean and stardust.

when it comes to attacking
the hell out of life and
making it your own,
there will never
be another her.

i am sorry for the ones before me that couldn't see
you for who you are. everything that makes you rare
and defined in your own skin, is what separates you
from those living in someone else's. you stand out
unlike any other woman who i have ever met in
my life.

to the way you bite your lip when you're thinking.
to the way you curl your hair to match the wind
around you.

there is a different type of circulation
of pureness inside your veins.

for every right and wrong choice

we make, we create a tomorrow

for ourselves by living and

dealing with the consequences

today.

i love how you count the raindrops
when you feel alone.

always know that everything in this
world has company, even when it is
an empty home.

-with you-

a possible life together is set before us. allowing you
and i the time to treasure all of the mountain's of love
in our hearts. one hand at a time. one breath at a time.
we will rise with them as each day brings new light into
our souls.

looking around, i am seeing a world that has lost
its way. in deep search for answers, i took a few
steps back, gathered my thoughts, and found
everything i had been looking for.

life found me when i was merely breathing.
you never know how many people would die
to have that breath you just took, until you
think it is a good idea to hold it in,
attempting to figure out others.

sometimes, you just have to
say, fuck it, and live without
limitations or boundaries.

there's always empty spaces
that need art.

she is everything i will ever need
in this life. just as the moon is
the only thing the sky needs
in order to uncover those
who have been kept in
the dark for too long,

she opens my windows and allows the light in.

there will always be a piece of you in
everyone i meet and in every place i
rest my wandering feet.

i hear you telling me to do my goddamn
best and showing me i am better than
those who have stolen what was
inside of my chest.

i will do this, because i know it's what
you would do.

from the first time we talked, my soul was already yours. sometimes, all it takes is for someone to come into your life not wanting to change you, but they just want to take a step forward with you. you might not have been able to trust yourself before, but now, someone else does.

darling, you are not only treasured,
you are an endless amount of hope
living in my bones.

allowing me the stability to finally
walk and not stumble over the
cities of doubt that had once
been in my way.

my love for you is the real kind. the kind that has the sea surrendering to the shore and breaking over it, time and time again in order to prove that everything is worth fighting for to be with the person you need.

if it can come back and find new ways to crash over the one thing it loves the most, i hope to wake up and find new ways to make a kiss and touch seem like they were invented just for us.

maybe all i will be is a voice to you.

but i hope it is one that leaves an

echo wherever you go.

when i told you that i loved you,

i meant it. somewhere in another

canyon of life, maybe i will be

able to hear yours as well.

no matter where i go and whoever might come into my
life, she will never be you. and for that reason alone,
i will be alone by choice until you are the only thing
i come home to.

-until my breath becomes
your breath, i will never
be at rest-

one of the hardest parts of life, is being judged for who you are not anymore. if i could give you any advice, it would be to never say you are sorry unless you absolutely meant it and when you tell someone you love them, make sure they know before it is too late.

countless people have been told and showed similar things before. make sure you are different than them, because this place is fucking cruel and people need someone they can trust.

together we discovered
a castle with walls
made form broken
bones and scar
tissue.

it wasn't as beautiful as
we were led to believe,
but the one thing we
did was never give
up on something
we considered
to be worth
more than
just the
cracks
that
were
showing.

we found home in each other and no matter the looks of it, we were safe because we had rebuilt what everyone kept trying to tear down.

over time, hate got in the
way of becoming who i
needed to be in order
to see over my own
eyes.

it had rested itself between
my heart and mind, and i
was never the same
again.

i was a king lost in his
own crown of doubt.

when the heart is running over with love
from the universe, its okay to drink from
it. you've earned it. value lessons and
know without pain, we would never
know the sweet taste of love we
were born to get drunk off of.

in the game of life and love, where your soul is constantly changing form, do not hesitate to soak in all the glory as you find yourself amongst the lost and forgotten. this is a crash course in a world where not everything makes sense and you will be a stranger to those around you because you were not made for this place.

> you are sick, but the truth is, we all are. some of us choose to be numb to the sin blooming inside of a heart we never want to break. while others remain open the entire time to the devastation and are okay feeling everything just to be alive.

she left with her spirit still intact.
no longer was it pinned to the
wall of her lover. too many times
it had been used for others things
besides love.

                    now it is hers again
                    to wear with pride.

there is great hope in the eye of the universe
for everyone that feels alone.

even the sky cannot contain its emotions and
has to release the fury and chaos of being
misunderstood.

> be gentle like rain.
> be strong like thunder.
> be brave like lightning
> as it continues to
> strike the heart
> of reason.

i took my toes and buried them into the sand of the gulf shores. it's my happy place. it's where i go when i'm in need of medication.

       a prescription only light can fill.

i jump from the sun to the moon to practice my ability to balance my energy. it's not practical, but it works for me while learning to regain the strength you took away.

you took my heart last night and thought it would
kill me, but i have the stars on my side.

they let me borrow a few to replace what you stole.

i plan on becoming more for them, while you are
busy losing yourself in the dark.

my grandfather passed away a few years ago and his last words to me were, "i love you." i think about it often and it allows me to fight every day for a cause i am willing to die for.

    i write because of pain. i write because not everyone has a chance to say what they are feeling.

        in death, i found life.
        in life, i found hope.
        in hope, i found words.
        in words, i found meaning.
        in meaning, i found you.

like a butterfly testing its wings for the first time,
she prepared herself for the initial flight of her
life.

she had to shed who she was for the betterment of
her spirit. she is now an adventure waiting to
happen, and the stars are all home now.

i have used this body on things that never understood me.

i have abused this soul on people who never loved me back.

i have days where the hardest thing i do is get out of bed, but each day i grow older, not in time, but in space.

and if i could tell her anything, it would be that she has loved me with a love unknown to me. a love so complete and true that the ones before her who told me the same words were only throwing up lies to see how they could make themselves feel better.

to bathe in a love like hers, has my soul drinking in the moon and all the magic falling from her lips.

your smile is something i have heard about before, but never saw with my own eyes. it was an idea in my head of how happy is supposed to look like, every time my windows are able to witness this endearing miracle. i wonder how it feels for you knowing you've injected acceptance into a heart that stopped beating a long time ago. if we ever argue, or have any ill feelings towards each other for whatever reason, i know at the end of the day, two bodies will be as one. love can be a lot of things, but most importantly, all it has to be is a smile that helps someone finally feel enough for once. it's in the simplest acts of the word itself that we find the most of who we are.

wherever you are, i will make it to you with the words,
"i do." not to have you for the rest of my life in the
way married couples think, but to have you know i am
dedicating my life towards you, for us. we have the
capability to become something more than the moon
and sun could ever be. we create the dreams others
cannot see. we hand the universe letters to read and
in return, it provides us the stars. i will forever write
for you, because i know nothing else but you, and i
want that to continue for as long as i am breathing
and even past my last breath.

> i will tell everyone about the human
> who turned a soul into a lover.

in this life, there are no mistakes when it comes to

forever. all it takes are two naked hearts that wish

to live it, while confiding in the other everything it

needs to beat fiercely and breaking open to find

the other inside. i took a chance on fate and it

had been you all this time who was beating

inside of my chest.

in order to change the world,
you must first create one for
yourself.

one where dreams are inhaled
and wild is produced.

one where there are no what ifs,
only defined purpose for each
action.

when i told you those things, i didn't lie to you.

tomorrow changes the soul just as the sun

and moon change the horizon.

no matter how hard the universe
tries to tell us, no, we need each
other. you and i, darling, are our
very own kind of love.

one that will not be torn apart by
the unforeseen nature that is
called life.

i
will
only
drown
for
those
who
can
see
beneath
the
surface.

her eyes are the reason
i fell in love with the
ocean in the first place.

the longer they stay
open, the more i
want to swim.

as close as two stars colliding,
we found meaning by
destroying who we
once were,

to become who we needed
to be for each other.

i feel so at peace with you here next to me.
i can vehemently tell you i've never had
this before.

this way of breathing is foreign to me. it's as
if my lungs finally tasted fresh air and knew
it was okay to expand around an idea of
something greater than what they were
meant to feel.

i am sorry for the ones before me that could never dance with you in the rain. but i will never be sorry for giving you all of the love that i had left to give in this life. i know some of it has been wasted and misused by others. i am sorry we couldn't have met before, when i had so much more than just words, but i am here now, and i am staying for the duration of our heartbeats.

it's how you hold your reflection that made me love you.

i knew if there ever came a time when i had a weak

moment, you'd help me up, and we would finish

what needed to be done.

i've never been one to be greedy, but tonight i am going to be.

i am wishing on the sky full of stars to one day feel your skin pressed against my arms.

people have asked me before what's my idea of heaven, and i tell them, it is you and me, sweet one.

age will never kill you, sweetheart.
you are too gorgeous of a soul for
even death to look at and think
otherwise.

what will happen though, is it will
want to fall in love with you, and
if i have to, i will fight to save
you from succumbing to
such an childish idea.

if you vibe with the same music,
you have a keeper and someone
who knows your soul as much as
the sounds that live within it.

i just have to laugh and i adore you because through it all,
you patiently just love me. no pressure. no expectations.
i feel loved with you. it's as if the sun finally rested on
the arms of the moon. it has been granted to all of
those who had nightmares about the ones they
loved not being there in the morning.

we are all human and can speak
without talking and learn without
reading.

we are the flowers in the wake of
spring, readying ourselves for the
next bloom of love.

-secrets-

i always wanted someone who would tell me a story.
i was afraid to go to sleep, but no one ever could
until i met you. you tell the best stories and settle
my soul to rest and my heart now knows of a
wild love.

i love you.

> you have this incredible soul and i need you. you are light, love, and comfort in human form. you are irreplaceable, unique, and you matter.

> you are so important in ways you cannot see or imagine. but i see it and one day you will see it as well.

> i know this because i see you catch tiny glimpses of it and it is beautiful to watch.

if i never see you again,
i now know your touch
and soul a little more.
i will try and find you
again in all of the
ways and places
you have always
seen me.

i've been watching you sleep,
because it's one of my favorite
things to do.

it is in that moment your breath
becomes mine, and i start my
day.

you are rare, beautiful, and kind.

to know you i feel like i have lived

a thousand lives with you.

> just know that each one is
> a new sunset kissing my
> eyes.

she wears darkness as a
princess wears her wings;
extremely confident,
beautiful, and above all
else, as if they were only
meant for her survival.

i am always with you.
regardless of what
you have in your
heart during
the storms,

i am there for you,
with you, as one
who loves you
through it.

    i am the sun that never leaves your life.

it's a feeling unlike anything i have ever felt before,
and to know it is you, i can come to you and spill
my stories. being able to have an open outlet,
allows me to rid my soul of the secrets it was
difficult keeping in for so long.

you are my constant north. you are my feet when
they are standing firm beneath me. you are my
eyes when they feel reason for opening.
you are a home that is constantly
filled with love.

you are my safest place in every room.

she loves this hard because her
life has taught her how it feels
to be cherished so little.

there's no replacing a broken
soul, but there are lessons to
be learned on how to heal
yourself, by being your
own magic.

women are not only the entirety of what makes us who we are, they are a complete and true circle, full of power to manifest, vibe, and heal everyone around them who thought life was meant to be experienced at half
the speed of believing.

she stole my heart with her
fingers on the keys and now
she sings for me the melodies
of the sea;

        -one wave at a time-

humans have a funny
way of choosing the
life they want.
when it comes down
to security, they will
for the most part,
always reach for
unhappiness,
over the uncertainty
that lies behind the
unknown.

if you ever find yourself where you do not feel
comfortable or wanted,

take a step back, assess the situation, breathe
in the wind, and decide if you want to share
that with the person you are with.

being alone is not a jail sentence. it is self-preservation.

we fall on our hearts, onto a dagger made from love.
hoping that through our sacrifice, we can find a
worthy reason for getting up again and feeling
the wound heal over time with the scar it
leaves behind telling how we survived
to make the most out of life.

you are love in immortal form.
there's no other way i have
ever seen you nor will
there be.

you are as pure as the waters
you allow me to drink from.

we write in code, and oftentimes we forget which
messages are intended for who. though we never
cross the same ones twice, we are able to digest
a universe within a single turn of our heart,
as it looks to move forward along the path
of the unknown.

it is there where we find the gumption to hold on
to everything others try and remove from us that
they think we don't need. if only they would do
the same thing to themselves maybe they would
understand how we have arrived when they
are still aimlessly wandering the world
alone.

she told me, "i love the way you talk to me. i cannot describe it and what it does to me. i am at a loss for words when you take them and my breath away."
i smiled as if the sun crept onto her shoulder and i was the only one who could see it. gently leaning into her, i whispered, "there is no description needed, lover. we both understand what it feels like to be inside the soul of the other without having to touch or say a single word. we move like water through an open creek, begging to be lost in the dimensions of the mountains surrounding it. finding each turn to be more riveting and full of endless motion to keep us moving towards the climax of every star born."

you don't get to be a living ghost.
you don't get to deprive and
punish your body any longer.

mind.   body.   spirit.

that is how the universe is connected and that is how
i love you. to be with you, i am tied to every end that
is you. you, my love, make me feel alive and worthy of
being held by arms, kissed by lips, touched by fingertips,
and loved in every way imaginable that pertains to
growing in all directions.

your vibrations are so strong and they
keep going for as far as the soul can
feel.

    i could sense you releasing, as you
    matched each move.

        there is no greater feeling than being
        inside of the heart you love the most.

she opened her legs for me, and i could see
every beginning to my life. it was there i
found our religion and i thank her daily
for allowing me to worship in each
breath we give to our chaos.

in her eyes
i found my
vision
and
it was as
clear
as the day
i found her
for the first
time.

you are my peace and clam.

holding you, i feel everything

i need to.

she watches over me
    with more dedication
        and love than the stars
    above me.

        i can only hope
           the sky can learn
                from her bravery.

-writing-

you must be willing to let out the pain so love can grow
where you once could not stop bleeding.

the paper understands better than people and it will always
be there to keep your hands steady.

whatever you want from life, make it a priority and turn
your journey into adventures. you never know what
could happen once you learn how to reach the
moon by believing it lives inside of you.

after that, you will be able to drink from the waterfalls
and dance in the falling skies you once only knew by
heartache.

if only we could see the fire
so many have been burned
by,

then maybe we would be
able to set ourselves free
from the ashes they
pretend to be.

live beyond the sounds of negativity you are surrounded by. tune out the noise by turning up your sense of wonderment.

live there. drink there. be love in every step.

that's the thing about us. no matter where she goes,
i will always be there with her. i not only love her,
but i trust who she is and what she believes in.
it's important to do so, because there is no
me without her. there is no center of my
world without her. there is not anywhere
left to go. the only destination is
together, because our love
taught me that.

where we go from here, is for us to decide.
wherever that is, may we find ourselves
in love, drunk in madness, and learning
from the wild we share for a chance to
be closer to the essence of each flower
that grows because of our dedication
to our own forever.

don't go through life afraid to take that next breath, or next step.

<u>create. build. overcome.</u>

greatness takes time, but for some of us, time is nothing more than an excuse people use when they run out of it.

though we may fall and lose
our minds at times, we have
been built by the universe
that collapses on itself
in order to be born
again of light and
love.

-always trust the stars-

walk with your heart
and tell it how much
the sun loves rising
for the beats it plays
as it shines for you.

however you see the day,
close your eyes when you
get a chance and you will
see every possibility
between you and the way
to them, as the soul comes
out of you.

break open your chest and air
out the negativity you may
have been keeping in.

the truth lies within the breath
we are at times too afraid to take.

there's no substituting passion
for anything less than the
insanity you embark on.

hold steady and push your lungs
out for a chance at true
happiness.

books shouldn't be the only place
you feel it.

to the tips of the stars there is only
more to discover. locate what it is
you need and devour everything,
including the soul.

you must always find a way to thrive.

across the bones of yesterday,
you will come to see how
complete you are.

there's great heart to be
discovered as long as
you move forward.

from here,

    we will move with

    the air from our

    dreams.

i come bearing my soul in the form of my naked love.
these flowers are from my bones and they are freshly
picked every day for you.

my falling star. my calm and peaceful seas.

you are the cure to all the lunacy
running rampant in the holes of
me.

my soul married your soul when we started over.
just as a new day brings the sun out of its dream,
you meet me where i need you to be;

                    at all times during the day.

even when all is left of the day is a single star welcoming the moon, i will look to the horizon of my life and open my eyes to take you in and hold you once again. one star will always be enough for me to know just how lucky i am to be alive and thankful for you tonight.

tired of what had been dragging her down, she turned over a new wave. approaching the end of the world, she kept swimming in hopes of catching that california sunshine and a peace of mind she knew existed.

stay creating and never stop. not for anyone. in order to live, you must be willing to breathe in the fire sometimes. allow it to fuel your passion. whatever it is. wherever you find it. fucking live it and do it with all of your heart and soul. life wasn't meant to be experienced going through the motions. stay focused and dream even if you're the only who can see it.

even though
we are apart,
the moon
continues
collecting our
dreams as we
fight on for
the stars.

out of the wild,
we bare our
wounds to
those who
thought
we'd never
make it.

believe in more than a
reason to quit and
you will be rewarded
by a soul who never
gives up on you.

looking up, i still wonder how it's possible to feel all of the universe when it's standing right next to you, a thousand miles away.

settle your nerves. be calm through the chaos.
hold everything you love deep within the
pockets of your soul.

                when you're ready, expose your truths.

there's a great possibility
in the world around you.

if you have a stubborn heart,
you'll never be without.

it's the greatest weapon one can possess.

never shade
your heart
from the
things that
bring out its
light.

-shine on, wild heart-

-go now-

> go where the universe inside
> of you calls and plant your
> soul and love in the energy
> underneath you.

some days it feels as if i can change the world and other days it's me changing myself. two constants are in my life; you and everything that is you. we sculpt our dreams by the actions we were once afraid to use.

like the salt in the sea,
we moved as one and
loved without
expectations.

    we were made to become the waves
    and roll throughout the open space.

love is finding yourself happy with or without them.

        once you realize this,
        you will have arrived
        at the point of never
        turning back to who
        you were.

deep down there is a purpose
growing inside of your soul.
find a place where it brings it
out without wanting more than
you can offer. there you will find
your mirror.

there is no explanation
for why things occur
in our hearts and not
in our minds.

                                        we just hope they agree that
                                        love is the most important
                                        battle.

go until your lungs are screaming.

go until your heart is crying out.

go until your soul is bleeding.

        go before it's too late.

open your eyes and
allow them to see
everything beautiful
and wild.

keep them steady
and love again.

follow your dreams even if no one else is there to help you. they are the stories our souls will tell in the next life.

those who do, will find it easier to close their eyes, when all too often they played hide and seek with your heart.

and that's how it happens. a wrong turn that turned out to be right. sleeping that extra hour and then getting dressed to go out. buying the wrong thing at the store then having to return it. staying a few extra minutes at the beach. wandering into a place you are unfamiliar with, only to find at the end of the day, it was everything that had ever felt normal.

breath in.

    rest there for a moment.

breathe out.

    move forward and feel
    everything you've been
    afraid of.

        <u>let go and seize the soul of today.</u>

we go where our
stars lead us and
i hope they lead
you somewhere
exquisite and
kind.

rotating around the world
of the unknown, we hope
to land on something strange
so we can feel alive and needed.

    we are all looking for our own fall.

i don't want to move and not feel your body next to mine.

it is the keeper of all my sanity and reason to keep trying.

it is my lifeline. it is my nightlight. it is my safe haven.

without it, i am no use to the hands i try to make a fist

with when the world is battling me for my desires.

use your voice.

> the time we have is precious, but what we do with it can become a guide to how others travel. we write lines so others can walk across knowing it's okay to fall and get back up before time calls us back.

always live with your heart
outside of your chest.

allow the universe to see inside.
allow it the love it needs.

life teaches us that we are better when we are kind to ourselves. remain the greatest love story to your soul. continue on despite what you are going through.

the things we learn will propel us into the sky without fearing anything below us.

-we are the birds of flight-

go with the wind and uproot your love as
you travel the lands and search for the
place of adventures that your fingertips
can feel.

keep giving yourself these little gems
and your chest will be a garden for
the gods who are in search of
mountains and oceans not
yet offered by mortals.

speak the lines inscribed on your heart
and you will see who will be there after
your story is told.

>	speak without trembling.
>	speak with conviction.
>	speak until you can hear
>	yourself.

you never know what you are
capable of until you let your
dreams breathe.

stay passionate about the
things you love and they
will make you proud.

hearts train the eyes and it's imperative to have them closed for a few seconds each day before you rest so it knows what it's fighting for tomorrow.

a day without you is a lifetime without love.

that is something i will never recover from.

they might as well bury me if that moment

ever comes.

-do what you love-

that's all you should ask form yourself.

that's all anyone should want for you.

it's okay not to know
the next part of your
life.

> you are here now.
> enjoy that and
> everything it
> brings.

we grow in darkness because we are the essence of what lives inside of us.

for those that do, i am proud of you.

keep going. keep living. stay you.

take what you've been through and help others.
be the path they can follow when lost is no
longer a direction needed, but felt by all
who embrace it.

do creative shit
and motivate
yourself in all
areas of your life.

repeat. repeat. repeat.

never recycle the old dreams
that kept you fearful of the
night.

we live.
we learn.

and somewhere in the middle we think we have it all figured out, until we get met by life at the most inopportune time and the earth is ripped from underneath us. it is then we will learn who we are and who we thought we were.

watching you
outside of my
dreams is the
most beautiful
thing my eyes
see during their
day out of my
head.

i'm too opened minded for the
closed doors others live behind.

if you aren't helping me grow,
you will be removed, along with
the rest of the weeds located
near my heart just begging for
attention and my energy.

believe in yourself.

love yourself.

know yourself.

be everything you
have went without.

now is everything.

now is the only
place you have.

each time you find yourself, know that you will have to duplicate this process throughout life. tomorrow will try and change you, but you have the power to change the day.

never forget where
your soul came
from.

       if you ever think about giving up,
       just remember how much it went
       through to get to you.

you have a right to feel everything your love desires. don't settle for normalcy when you were made for the wicked nights and screaming seas of another world.

if you try and
get in the way
of my dreams,
you'll be the
reason why
you're no
longer a part
of them.

as your feet begin to move with the rotations of the earth, never be afraid to fall from the gravity. it is during this brief encounter, you will decide to hold on, or let go.

-i hope your hands release the fear-

don't confuse someone's
attention as love.

they will show you
the difference.

do what you love and if
anyone you care about
doesn't support you,

    leave them there.

i'm not looking for a ticket.
just a seat in front and maybe
she looks at me and if she
doesn't, then i am still learning
more about myself and what i
need to do in order to get better
at giving more of my time to
myself.

love comes and goes they say,
but if it touches the roots of
the soul, there it will stay
and produce the magic
we see in our dreams.

go wherever your heart kisses
the moon and where your
bones can feel the stars.

-keep fighting-

you exist for a greater purpose.
you belong to more than an
idea of being someone who
deserves less than anyone
else.

it's the second day of the new year and i am wondering
what the new me is supposed to be like down the road.
i wonder if he will think the same and love the same.
i wonder if he will know the same names as he does
now and if the people he calls his friends will still be
around. it's the second day of the new year, and it all
still feels the same, but there's reason to think things
will get better, even if the ideas are a bit rusty and
scattered amongst the clouds. i wonder if he will see the
old me and laugh at how foolish he was all of those years
for never believing in himself, or if he will keep walking
and not give it any thought. whoever he is and wherever
he goes, there's reason for me to think he will know what
to do when looking forward into his life and stops looking
back at everything that went wrong and accept they have
put in him in the new state of mind his heart needs to
write and live by.

this enchanting road.

>   the one i thought i had been walking alone all this time. it's where you have always been. i just had to walk a little further by myself in order to truly find love. the kind that never leaves you. the kind that wraps you up and keeps you safe. the kind that releases your mind and spirit from yesterday's chains. the kind that makes you want to marry the randomness of a person, because it makes you feel whole and important. i will love you with all the love inside of me, until there is nothing left but flowers growing where my heart used to be. even then, it will still be alive.

sometimes i take for granted just how fucking lucky i am. knowing i get to look at this every day, while others are rummaging though dumpsters and who knows what else in order to find something to eat. how some people move from shelter to shelter just to find a place to call home for the night. i met this kid, this young boy one time, i believe he was eight years old. he was a double amputee. i saw the joy in his face, with a smile that lit up my soul. he was not mad or angry at the world, he was simply happy. at such a young age he knew how much better he had it than most. even if he didn't have everything at that moment, he had his life. always enjoy your time here. always find a reason to smile and laugh and hurt yourself while doing both of those things. it's worth it. i promise. there is no other feeling like that of having the pleasure of knowing hardships, but never conceding to them.

there's a map on the back of
your dreams that you must
never forget about. it's there
for your soul to find you
when it goes in search of the
stars.

go where the sun

kisses the moon

and find yourself

in the greatest

bloom of life.

you have become my sanctuary for all things that need love. i am going to rest my entire life inside of you. i am going to try to take up every inch of your being and become the man you have told me i always could be. you didn't believe me when i told you that i loved you after only two months, but it was the day after we talked i knew my heart would end up in your hands. we all have a moment of complete nirvana, where souls align and touch each other in a way that brings peace and calm into the storm of everything we had done prior to meeting. you are the name of each star and galaxy existing within these very humbled bones of a man. closing my eyes, i not only see the world differently, i see you as before, when we were lovers in another time.

www.ingramcontent.com/pod-product-compliance
Lightning Source LLC
Chambersburg PA
CBHW032029290426
44110CB00012B/723